MEDIEVAL
TOWN AND COUNTRY LIFE

EMMA JOHNSON

W

FRANKLIN WATTS
LONDON • SYDNEY

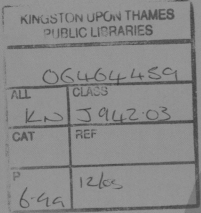

This edition 2003

Franklin Watts
96 Leonard Street
London
EC2A 4XD

Franklin Watts Australia
45-51 Huntley Street
Alexandria
NSW 2015

Illustrations David Frankland/Lee Montgomery (p.6)
Designer Billin Design Solutions
Editor Caroline Brooke Johnson
Art Direction Jason Anscomb
Editor-in-Chief John C. Miles

A CIP catalogue record
for this book is available
from the British Library.

Dewey classification: 942.03

ISBN 0 7496 5190 3

Printed in Hong Kong/China

Kingston Libraries

This item can be returned
or renewed at a Kingston
Borough Library on or
before the latest date
stamped below. If the item
is not reserved by another
reader it may be renewed
by telephone up to a
maximum of three times by
quoting your membership
number. Only items issued
for the standard three-week
loan period are renewable.

www.kingston.gov.uk/libraries

Royal
Kingston

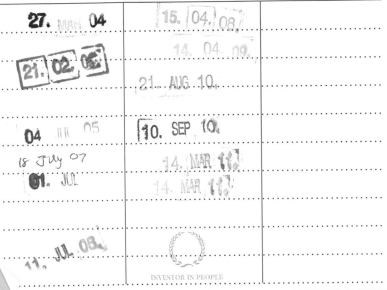

CONTENTS

All change!

When the Roman Empire collapsed in the 5th century AD, land-hungry Germanic tribes pushed across Europe, looting Roman towns and estates. Over time, separate kingdoms emerged; these brought more orderly rule to much of Europe. This stability heralded the beginning of the historical era known as the Middle Ages, or the medieval period.

COUNTRY AND TOWN

At the time of the Germanic invasions, most people lived in the countryside, labouring on farms and smallholdings. This rural population was swelled with refugees from the ruined towns. While some Roman towns survived, new settlements, founded by the invaders, sprang up across all of Europe.

A NEW STRUCTURE

By AD 800, Europe was a more stable and prosperous place. Christianity had become widespread, playing a major part in society.

Kings and nobles began to commission the building of churches and the rising population was soon divided into parishes.

THE BITERS BIT

The Franks and Saxons, who evolved into the French and English, now experienced the destruction of their own settlements. These were burnt and looted by pagan warriors from Scandinavia who became known as the Vikings. The Vikings sailed their superbly built ships down the English Channel in search of new territory.

Norman knights, such as this one, were descendants of Viking warriors.

> **"While the King was away, Bishop Odo built castles throughout the land, oppressing the unhappy people, and things went ever from bad to worse."**
> The *Anglo-Saxon Chronicle*

Initially raiders, Vikings over time settled and built towns in areas near the coasts and on the river estuaries of Britain, Ireland and northern France.

The chief invaders of England were from Denmark, and the part of England they conquered became known as the Danelaw. This area included much of what is today eastern England. In France, the duchy of Normandy was created by Rollo, a Viking who became the first Duke of Normandy in 911.

NEWS REPORTERS
The first written records of life in the towns and villages of Europe were made by chroniclers. In their diaries, or chronicles, these medieval reporters wrote of important events, such as coronations and deaths of kings as well as disasters such as plague and famine.

Often, chroniclers included other events that interested them. Together with official documents such as the *Domesday Book* in England, chroniclers provide us with key information about early medieval life.

The best-known record of the time, the *Anglo-Saxon Chronicle*, was commissioned by King Alfred the Great in 891, at the start of his reign. It was eventually completed in 1154.

WILLIAM THE CONQUEROR

William was the illegitimate son of Robert the Devil, Duke of Normandy, and a tanner's daughter from Rouen in France. Most of his early life was spent fighting for his right to become Duke in place of his father. Normandy's position was precarious, with the threat of invasions from France to the south, Burgundy to the east and the Celtic state of Brittany to the west. Much of William's energy was spent defending the land he held.

Edward the Confessor, King of England, promised to make William his successor, but this pledge went against the will of Edward's subjects, who did not want a foreign lord. William invaded England in September 1066. He defeated Harold, the last English King, near Hastings and was crowned King the following year. He died during a battle in 1087.

The feudal system

Across Europe, medieval rulers instituted a strict social hierarchy known as the feudal system, based on land ownership and obligations. It governed every aspect of medieval life.

> ## "Not one cow, nor one pig escaped his attention."
> **Chronicler of the *Domesday Book***

A LANDOWNER'S DUTY

The king, as overall ruler, decided how much land a lord could own. In return, the lord gave "service" to his overlord, the king. The liability of a noble's service depended on how much land he was granted. Usually this meant that he had to provide the king with 40 days' military service each year and a number of knights. Failing that, the nobles had to give the king money so that he could hire mercenaries (paid troops). As the Middle Ages progressed, nobles increasingly paid a tax instead of knightly service.

A TENANT'S DUTY

Landowners — whether the nobles or the Church — were owed a service of labour from the tenants of their estates. This system ensured a cheap workforce — in many cases slave labour — and generated wealth for the nobility. It also bought secular landowners time to indulge in their hobby of continuous petty warfare.

A HARD LIFE

The lowest strata of medieval society, the peasants, accounted for more than 90% of the population. They were largely treated with contempt by the monarch and nobles. Their harsh life in the fields gave them little time to do anything but survive.

WORK

Although everybody worked in medieval times, very few people were actually paid for what they did. They worked in exchange for food, goods or the services of others. This resulted in an economy based on barter rather than money.

Key exceptions to this rule were merchants and craftsmen in towns and mercenaries hired by the king in times of war. Usually a knight's daily wage would pay a peasant for two years' labour.

NORMAN RULE

When the Normans invaded England in 1066, older ways of life for people in both town and country changed forever. For example, the Normans destroyed many towns and villages. Some were burnt, while others were pulled down and the materials used to build royal castles.

To create the Royal forests, William the Conqueror demolished entire communities and later introduced harsh forest laws. People caught poaching could be blinded or have their tongues cut out.

Norman rule, with its emphasis on centralized control, was stricter than Saxon rule. In Saxon times, peasants took grievances to local courts, or "folk moots". The Normans did away with this system and became generally more oppressive landlords.

At the centre of the feudal system was the oath of fealty, when a man put his hands between those of his lord and promised to "be his man", or faithfully serve him.

DOMESDAY BOOK

This record of English land ownership, tenants and possessions was commissioned by William the Conqueror and completed in 1086. William sent his "surveyors" around the country to find out how much farmland, woodland and pasture there was, who owned it, how many people lived there and how many mills, ploughs and livestock there were. The name of each place, town and village was recorded. The survey showed that most people lived in villages, as the majority of towns had less than 1,000 inhabitants.

The purpose of the *Domesday Book* was to reveal how much the country was worth so that William could set taxes and work out how many men it could provide for his army. Ironically, William the Conqueror could not read!

Kings and castles

Kings and queens lived at the top of the medieval social tree. They may have possessed wealth and status but, following the splendour of their coronation, their lives could be uncertain, brutal and all too often short.

A SECURE HOME

Norman monarchs built wooden castles to provide defensive positions for themselves and their followers. These early castles are known as "motte-and-bailey" castles. The main stronghold (keep) was built on an earth mound (motte). At its foot a protective stockade called a bailey surrounded other buildings. Eventually stone castles replaced these structures, dominating the surrounding countryside.

TOWNS FORM

Castles built by the monarch often became the "keystone" for the formation of a town or village. People built their dwellings near the fortifications so that they could flee to safety in times of danger. Towns developed as more and more houses were built. The towns were eventually surrounded by walls that extended from the fortress.

This manuscript painting shows a medieval coronation procession.

"Uneasy lies the head that wears the crown."

Shakespeare's Henry IV, Part II

CHARTERS

Once a town had grown, the King could grant it a charter. Charters freed towns to run their own affairs and to hold markets. This was encouraged by the King because taxes levied on goods sold meant more royal income.

LAW AND ORDER

Monarchs also had power over law and order (except in freed towns, which had their own justices).

Wealthy nobles often went unpunished for their crimes, except for treason, which carried the death penalty. Commoners suffered the most — executions, mutilations and brandings were common punishments for a wide range of offences.

A MONARCH'S LIFE

A medieval king such as Henry II of England (1133-89) would have enjoyed hunting, feasting and reading books.

He would have known many languages, including Latin. Access to these pleasures and pastimes was one of the advantages of being a monarch. But kings and queens had no recourse to special remedies for diseases. Monarchs were as likely as their subjects to die young.

Medieval queens were often powerful in their own right. Examples include the empress Matilda, mother of Henry II, and Henry's wife Eleanor of Aquitaine. Both these women had great influence and were far from meek and subservient.

ELEANOR

Forceful, beautiful and talented Eleanor of Aquitaine (1122?-1204) was an ideal match for her husband, Henry II. She travelled with Henry around his realms and became a patron of the arts, influencing 12th-century cultural life as much as politics. At least two of her children — Richard the Lionheart of England and Blanche, Queen of France — inherited her love of music, art and architecture. Henry was forced to imprison his ambitious wife for 16 years to prevent her from taking control of his dominions.

CASTLES AND KINGS

• To begin with, castles are built as garrisons and fortified centres for controlling people and repelling enemies

• Later, castles become residences for the king or his lords, with bed chambers, dining halls, chapels and household stores

• The first castles are simple rectangular towers. These develop into motte-and-bailey castles — wooden towers built on an earth mound, surrounded by a moat

• In the 1100s, a stone wall enclosing the mound is called a shell keep. From about 1200, concentric castles (enclosed by rings of walls) are built for extra fortification

• Before family or "house" names, medieval rulers are described in terms of their appearance or character. Charles III, King of the Franks, is known as Charles the Fat and Richard I of England is nicknamed "the Lionheart"

• The first royal family name is Plantagenet, coined for Geoffrey of Anjou, who wears a sprig of broom (Latin *Planta genesta*) in his cap

A powerful Church

By the 11th century the Christian Church, with the Pope in Rome as its leader, had become the unifying structure of the western world.

"The Land is white with churches."
12th-century chronicler

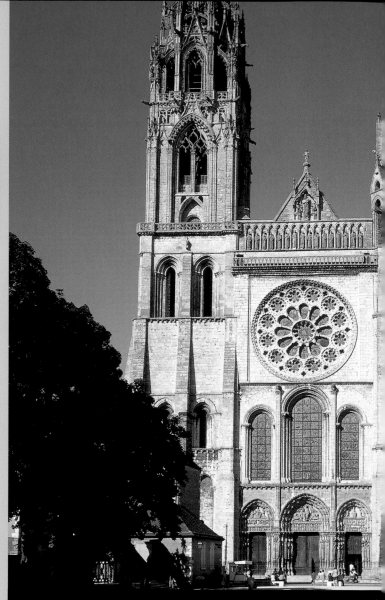

Cathedrals such as this one were built over generations.

RELIGION, WEALTH AND POWER

From humble beginnings, the Church had become materially and politically powerful. It owned huge tracts of land and large amounts of property in towns. Lands and possessions were willed to the Church by kings and nobles over many generations.

Church-owned properties in towns and the countryside were let out to tenants and the rents from these, paid in money and goods, helped to ensure that the Church's wealth rivalled that of the monarch's. This rivalry meant that power struggles often occurred between medieval kings and the Church's representatives, for example between King Henry II of England and Thomas à Becket in the mid-12th century.

At the beginning of the 13th century, Henry's son King John also clashed with the Church. As a result, England was put under interdict by the Pope. This meant that churches were closed and services suspended until John eventually surrendered. The Church possessed a powerful weapon in holding the key to life after death.

A KINGDOM WITH MANY HOUSES

Many different orders of monks and nuns were founded in the Middle Ages. Members of these orders dedicated their lives to Christ and lived according to rules they felt would please God. They spent their lives in work and prayer. Each order had churches, monasteries and/or nunneries, most of which were self-sufficient.

Such was the religious fervour of the times that whole generations of builders were dedicated to creating these places of worship. People engaged in this activity knew no other way of life.

CHURCHES

The Normans liked grand buildings; in Britain they wanted their own style to replace that of the conquered Saxons. By 1200, almost every Saxon cathedral and abbey had been demolished and the majority of smaller Saxon churches reconstructed.

In medieval times, even a small country church would have been colourful inside, with wall paintings and stained glass depicting biblical scenes. The priest read the Mass in Latin, which most of the congregation could not understand, although the words would have been familiar to them.

Few churches had seats, so people sat on the floor and listened to the priest.

THE CRUSADES

In 1095, Pope Urban appealed to Christian religious zeal when he preached the need for a Crusade, or war, against non-Christians. The first Crusade involved knights from all over Europe, including Britain.

The Crusaders captured Jerusalem and set up a kingdom in Palestine known as *Outremer*. The stated aim of the the Crusades was to allow Christians to make pilgrimages to the Holy Land. By 1291, there had been six Crusades, which produced no other result than a unified Muslim world, set against enemies of the Islamic faith.

BUILDING FOR GOD
Church buildings grew larger and more elaborate as the Middle Ages went on. Some cathedrals took hundreds of years to complete.

BECKET

A close friend of King Henry II, Thomas à Becket was appointed Archbishop of Canterbury (the highest English Church office) in 1162. He often clashed with the King as Henry repeatedly challenged the authority of the Church. When Becket returned from exile in France in 1170, he excommunicated (barred from the Christian Church) some of his bishops who had sided with the King. Henry was furious and sent four knights to speak to the Archbishop.

Historians are uncertain about what happened next, but the result was the murder of Thomas on 29 December 1170. Three years later, Becket was made a saint. His tomb became an important medieval place of pilgrimage.

Everyday religion

Christianity supplanted many older, pagan religions and used cunning as well as Christ's message of love and salvation to win the people over to its side.

> "My father, weeping, gave me a weeping child, into the care of the monk Reginald, and sent me away into exile for the love of God, and never saw me again."
>
> **Orderic Vitalis, a Norman monk**

CENTRE OF LIFE

The lives of most people in medieval times were dominated by the Church, which provided a meeting place as well as a centre for spiritual comfort, healing, education and entertainment.

In a small, poor village, the priest depended on the villagers for his daily meals and sometimes even the roof over his head. In larger, prosperous towns rich merchants sometimes made offerings to "God and the Church" to help them in business or for priests to pray for their souls after death.

THE CARING CHURCH

Hospitals and schools were run by the Church, and basic care of the sick was undertaken by monks and nuns of nursing orders. Treatments were based on herbal remedies, although some physicians performed basic operations, during which the patient would be dosed with poppy to help control the pain.

Monks were often the only people in the community who could read and write, and they taught in schools established by the Church. Churches also offered sanctuary to any offender who crossed their threshold. It was illegal to try to arrest someone once they were on "holy ground".

HOLIDAYS

Town and country people celebrated holy days (holidays) and feast-days. These special occasions included Christ's birthday — lasting from Christmas Day until 6 January — days that recognized saints' lives and events such as the harvest.

Passion plays, re-enactments of stories from the Bible, were performed by the people of a village or a town guild (an association similar to a trade union), and these were very popular.

AGE OF FAITH

People from all walks of life went on pilgrimages, journeying to holy places to pray for a favour or to show their devotion to God. Many churches displayed "relics". These were bones, body parts and possessions of various Christian saints. People believed that by praying at shrines where relics were held their prayers would be answered.

Pilgrimage routes spread across Europe from one town to another, with the most "holy" destinations at Canterbury, Rome, Santiago de Compostela in Spain and the Holy Land itself. Some people used a pilgrimage as an excuse to leave home and travel with friends. This may have been the case with Chaucer's pilgrims in *The Canterbury Tales*, written in the 1300s.

A medieval-style passion play dramatizing the life of Christ is stll performed every ten years at Oberammergau, in southern Germany.

FACT FILE

RELIGIOUS TIMES

• Dates are hard to fix in medieval times as they relate to religious festivals. The year begins at Easter, and so New Year's Day is not the first day of January, but March 25, the feast of the Annunciation of the Blessed Virgin Mary

• Time is fixed according to the Offices (prayer services) of the Church. Midnight until dawn is called Prime, morning is Tierce, afternoon is Nones and evening is Compline

• Until the early 11th century, priests can marry. The more unworldly monks of the Cluniac order ban this practice and the tradition of celibate monks is established

• A tithe is a tax of one-tenth of the annual produce or labour taken to support the church. Tithes paid in corn or foodstuffs are housed in a tithe barn

• Church courts exist alongside lay courts and are supposed to try only cases relating to spiritual matters. However the two types of courts often compete for jurisdiction over offences

A SERIOUS AFFAIR

For most pilgrims, though, going on a pilgrimage was a serious business. Perhaps they went to make amends for their sins, or in search of a cure for a disease.

Some may just have had a burning desire to see the holy places.

Whatever the reason, for many pilgrims it was their first time away from their town or village.

Some fared badly, being robbed or starving before they reached their destination; others met new people and were offered help along the way, experiencing the journey of a lifetime.

Nobles

A noble's ancestors were often warriors who had managed to make a good living through violence and robbery. Their more socially acceptable descendants – barons and knights – lived near the top of medieval society.

> **"Because that knights, squires and gentlemen go upon journeys and follow the wars, it beseemeth wives to be wise in all they do, for that most often they dwell at home without their husbands who are at court or in divers lands."**
>
> The *Book of Three Virtues* by Christine de Pisan, 1406

NOBLE DUTIES

Many nobles lived by the sword and spent much of their lives in battle. Fighting was a nobleman's substitute for work. He was also supposed to protect those beneath him socially, and for this he earned exemption from certain taxes.

As a wealthy landowner, a noble exercised authority over the peasants who lived and worked for him, controlling every aspect of their lives.

Service and loyalty in exchange for protection, justice and order was the medieval way.

COURT AND COUNTRY

The most powerful nobles – the barons – advised the monarch on matters of state. Lesser nobles, such as dukes, earls or counts, took part in local government. They often became sheriffs of the shire or county in which they lived. Their duties included collecting taxes for the king.

The successful noble would be able both to hold his own on the battlefield and to be amusing company at the royal court, which was always on the move from town to town. Courtiers spent much of their time making alliances with whoever had enough power to maintain or advance their position within the nobility.

Life was more relaxed in the country, where hunting game, hawking and feasting were a noble's main pastimes.

Other leisure pursuits included playing chess, dice and backgammon. A noble's country business involved overseeing his estate and making sure his tenants were paying their rents and taxes.

A WOMAN'S PLACE

A noblewoman's life was much more restricted. Her main purpose was to provide a male heir to carry on the family name. There were few outlets for a woman's energies and much of her time was spent alone, either supervising domestic servants or pursuing hobbies such as embroidery or music.

As chatelaine, or mistress of the house, she was in charge of running the estate in the lord's absence and, in exceptional circumstances, such as war, the defence of the castle or home.

THE MANOR FARM

In the countryside, land was divided into manors. The lord or lady of the manor was a noble, who owed his or her title to a more powerful landowner, such as a baron. The land that came with a manor, known as the demesne, might include more than one village.

Likewise, a village might owe allegiance (and rents) to more than one manor. The manor would also include a church and some surrounding farmland. The peasants attached to the manor worked the owner's land in return for a roof over their heads and land on which to grow food.

The lord appointed various officials from among the peasantry for the everyday running of the manor. The manor house was often a two-storey building with storage rooms on the ground floor and living rooms on the first floor. Sometimes it had a tower or moat as fortification.

A manuscript painting showing nobles out hunting.

Moving up

Status in society was not fixed. It was possible to become a member of the nobility if you had enough money and the right connections.

> ## "I thought I would be the only Queen here, but I find six hundred others."
>
> **Jeanne, wife of Philip the Fair of France, when she visited Bruges and saw how the merchants' wives were dressed**

Nobles dressed in the height of fashion.

THE NEW RICH

As time passed, towns and cities became more important. Lawyers and merchants moved into towns to provide services for the people who lived there.

In a typical medieval town about half the adult male population were either merchants or craftsmen. Many became very rich indeed. As they grew successful and wealthy, they paid more taxes, adding to the wealth of their kings, princes and nobles.

A TOWN HOUSE

A typical merchant's town house consisted of three floors, with a main hall on the first for dining and entertaining, family rooms and bedrooms on the second, and servants' rooms at the top.

A rich merchant living in a town could buy land in the country and marry his children into the nobility. He could even apply to the King's Herald for his own coat-of-arms and join the nobility himself.

MONEY, NOT LOVE

Few wealthy people married for love, as medieval marriages added to the power and wealth of the families involved. Large dowries (a cash payment to the husband's family at the time of marriage) had to be found for daughters.

Noble families on the edge of financial ruin welcomed a dowry from a wealthy merchant if it meant they could keep their noble status. In return, the merchant's status and influence increased.

MEDIEVAL ATTITUDES

• Most male nobles marry late, when they are over 30. Generally women marry earlier, in their teens or twenties

• Some girls are betrothed as young as seven, when they are "promised" for marriage in the future

• In the country, it is possible for an enterprising peasant to buy his freedom, acquire land and tenants of his own, marry a squire's daughter and become a noble himself. This is exceptional, but not unheard of

• Privacy is almost an unknown state – a master and mistress often share their bed with their household servants or guests, and travellers might be forced to share a bed with complete strangers

A noble who became so poor that he had to sell his armour and war horse and earn his living could be removed from the list of nobility. A noble who could not produce a male heir would also have his name removed from the rolls of the nobility upon his death.

CLOTHING LAWS

In medieval times the clothes you wore indicated your status. Sumptuary (from the Latin sumptus meaning "cost") laws were passed to attempt to regulate the kind of clothes people could wear. Peasants were often restricted to wearing brown or black; only nobles could wear furs, pointed shoes and hanging sleeves.

According to an English law of 1363, a merchant worth £1,000 could wear the same dress and eat the same meals as a knight worth £500. In other words a knight was twice as "noble" as a merchant. In the end, sumptuary laws were unenforceable – officials were unwilling to chase people through the streets to stop them wearing a particular item of clothing.

Knights

Armoured knights on horseback were the medieval equivalent of modern tanks. Their role in warfare was to act as shock troops, crushing the opposition by charging through the enemy's line. To do this, they used the weight of their armour and horses.

> **"Not one of us had a father who died at home. All have died in the battle of cold steel."**
> 13th-century French knight's song

English and French knights clash in battle.

APPRENTICE KNIGHT
Being a knight was a way of life — without his horse and sword, a knight was simply a soldier. At seven years of age, a noble boy was sent as a page, or trainee knight, to a castle, where he learned about a knight's way of life.

Being able to play a musical instrument, sing, dance and write were considered social assets for a knight. He also learned about table manners and personal hygiene.

Most importantly, he was trained to handle a horse and to use weapons. Strenuous physical exercises included running in full armour and practising with weapons that were twice the weight of those used in battle.

SOLDIER MONKS
Many knights joined military and religious orders such as the Templars, the Knights of St John and the Knights of the Teutonic Order to become soldier-monks.

These orders were heavily involved in the Crusades. Their headquarters were in towns, the most famous being the Knights Templars in Paris. In 1307, the order was outlawed.

King Philip the Fair of France based this action on trumped-up charges of sorcery. The vast store of treasure accumulated by the Templars over 200 years became the property of the King.

Chivalry came to embody the qualities of the perfect knight — loyalty, bravery and courtesy. Knighthood, with chivalry as its code of practice, was a kind of military guild in which all knights must be prepared to lay down their lives for each other or their king.

END OF THE ROAD
French knights were decimated by English archers at the battles of Crécy (1346) and Poitiers (1356).

After these battles, knights could no longer claim to be supreme warriors. They left most of the hard work of defending and attacking towns to the ordinary man-at-arms, since this activity did not appeal to a knight's natural inclination, which was for mounted combat.

WILLIAM MARSHAL

William Marshal started his career as a poor landless knight. At first he made his living winning ransoms or selling the armour and horses of the knights he beat in organized tournaments (he was a kind of medieval prize-fighter).

He was so successful at this that King Henry II and Queen Eleanor noticed him and rewarded him accordingly, appointing him a marshal in their service. By the time he died, in 1219, he had served three kings and had been made 1st Earl of Pembroke.

THE KNIGHT'S CODE
Chivalry was regarded as the way of life for all Christian knights. The word comes from the French *chévalerie*, meaning horsemanship or knighthood.

KNIGHTLY TRADITIONS

• A knight's sword is a symbol of his importance. His stone tomb effigy shows him with his sword

• A page becomes a squire aged 14 and goes into battle with his knight. If successful, at 21 he becomes a knight in his own right, at a ceremony in which he receives a heavy sword blow

• By the 15th century, a knight's iron and steel armour weighs about 20 kg (45 lb). A knight is able to run, mount a horse and lie down in armour

• Sometimes it becomes unbearably hot inside armour. Cloth is worn over the armour to keep it cool

• A knight's coat-of-arms is passed to his eldest son on his death

• Knights never ride a mare or in carriages since these are against the rules of chivalry

• Knights and noble squires receive a fixed salary, which is reviewed from time to time to make sure that they are deserving

• In the 14th century, as chivalry declines, knighthood seems to have "gone soft". There is growing evidence of comforts on campaign

Men-at-arms

A 14th-century battle scene showing men-at-arms in action at the siege of a town.

The professional soldier became increasingly important as the medieval age drew to a close, and it became clear that war could be a profitable business for a soldier who knew what he was doing.

"The Goddam and his crooked stick."

French knight's opinion of the English longbowman

PAID SOLDIERS

There had always been paid soldiers, but these were the exception rather than the rule in the Middle Ages. With the start of what was to become the Hundred Years' War (1346-1453) between England and France, more highly trained troops were sought by the opposing sides.

CHANGING ROLE

As the knights' effectiveness on the battlefield declined, paid soldiers provided the specialized skills necessary to win battles. They did not possess the knights' attitude that certain activities were beneath them, so they learned to use many different weapons.

These included the pike, the crossbow and the newfangled guns that came into use in the mid-14th century.

REWARDS

Common soldiers could expect little mercy in defeat, but this was a small drawback. A lucky man might capture a noble on the battlefield and be able to retire in luxury on the ransom his family paid.

In 1415, a mercenary was able to demand a wage of sixpence (2.5 new pence) a day — not bad when a family's food bill for a year might come to less than a pound!

The man-at-arms' motto was "work hard, play hard" and towns were important centres for recreation. Taverns did a roaring trade with soldiers who had gold in their pockets. Tradesmen did well too, as clothes, boots, weapons and equipment always needed replacing or repairing.

SIEGES

During sieges of castles or towns, men-at-arms were essential. They dug ditches and mines to collapse the town's walls, and gunners battered the walls to create a breach through which the army could enter.

RUTHLESS

In the field, troops were expected to live off the land — the peasants suffered and starved as invading armies took their precious crops and animals.

If a town surrendered without a fight, the lives of people within the walls would probably be spared, but otherwise no quarter was given. The defenders could be slaughtered and their property looted by the victors.

Once ordinary soldiers began working for money, warfare became a much more ruthless business.

FREE COMPANIES

During intervals of peace in the Hundred Years' War (1346–1453), bands of discharged soldiers called free companies roamed Europe looking for employment. These men had their own leaders, such as Sir John Hawkwood (left). They hired themselves out to fight for anyone who paid enough. In between jobs, they took over towns and strongholds or terrorized local communities, extorting whatever they could. Attempts were made to get rid of these anarchic groups, including the use of bribes. Eventually, Italy absorbed most of the free companies during the wars between various city-states.

Freemen

In between nobles and peasants, there were freemen or sokemen – smallholders independent of a lord. They were free to put themselves under the protection of a lord or, if skilled, to work profitably in a town.

"In the name of God and of profit."

Motto on an Italian merchant's ledger

FREEMAN

A freeman's or a freewoman's condition was not far removed from that of a peasant's. But his or her status in society was different.

It was a principle of medieval life that every man and woman must have a lord. The "free" title meant that land belonging to a freeman could not be treated as a noble's possession.

A freeman could voluntarily put himself and his land under the protection of a noble. Unlike a serf, he was free to move from place to place.

FREEMEN IN TOWNS

Cities and towns were centres of trade in which freemen could thrive. Since everything was made by hand, craft workers became very important.

Typical craft skills included stone carving, glazing, carpentry, processing wool, coin making, glass blowing, potting and metal working.

Craft workers and traders made a reasonable living. Guilds, associations and brotherhoods grew up to help traders and craft workers and to protect their businesses from competition.

Busy craft workshops in a typical late-medieval town.

People who worked at the same trade tended to live close together and, at a time when few people could read, large wooden signs representing the various trades were hung outside workplaces.

A young person who wished to learn a particular trade could be made an apprentice, or trainee craft worker. Apprentices were supervised by master craftsmen, who were responsible for the quality of their work.

RICHES OF TRADE

As the Middle Ages progressed, town wealth was generated through trade in luxuries such as jewels, spices and silks.

Italian merchant companies began to operate as banks in market towns, issuing credit notes to merchants, nobles and even to royalty.

By 1400, weaving workshops in towns provided jobs for many people and, in England, woollen cloth was a major export.

Wool bales were checked by customs officials before they left the country and stamped with a wool-growers' guild seal and a customs seal.

SUPPORTIVE GUILDS

Every event in the lives of craft workers was supported by the guilds. They provided charity for those in need, as well as a chance to take part in entertainments, such as passion plays. As guilds grew richer, they built impressive guildhalls for ceremonial occasions.

FACT FILE

ENGLISH TOWN AND COUNTRY FREEMEN

• More than 14,000 freemen and 23,000 sokemen hold land in 1086, 80% in the Danelaw (eastern England)

• A member of the "free" class usually owns about eight hectares (20 acres) of arable land

• The term "sokeman" comes from "soke", the name of a district under a particular administration

• There are probably a large number of women smallholders, who lie hidden in the records of *Domesday* because masculine wording is used throughout

• Street names in towns and cities often reflect the trades that take place there, such as Candlemaker's Row and Bread Street in London

• Large towns hold a market every day, except for Sunday, and people sell food and livestock on their stalls. In smaller towns, the market takes place at least once a week

MEDIEVAL WHO'S WHO

REEVE – a caretaker of the manor in the lord's absence. A reeve usually had some other job – perhaps he was the local miller – and lived in his own home with his family. He also organized work for the villagers on the lord's land, sold crops, and suggested plantings.

FRANKLIN – landowner who was free, but not of noble birth.

FREEMAN – a freeman did not have to live and work on the lord's land, but was free to go wherever he wanted.

VILLEIN (from the Latin villa, meaning "house") – a villager attached to a manor farm, who had to work for the lord in return for a house, garden, and some land of his own, which he kept for his lifetime. Whoever took over the land when the villein died had to give the landlord his best animal as a fee.

COTTAGER – like a villein, a cottager was not allowed to leave the village. He had to promise to work for the lord for six or seven days a year, mainly during the harvest, and in return was given a cottage and garden for his lifetime, but no land.

Peasants

At the bottom of the social ladder were peasants and serfs. They were mainly country folk, whose lives tended to be harsh and short.

> **"Good people, nothing can go well in England unless there is neither villein nor nobleman."**
>
> John Ball, Yorkshire priest, to rebel peasants in 1381

PEASANTS

Although this group of people was the most numerous and their labour provided food for all, they were treated with contempt by most nobles and the emerging middle classes.

Peasants generally belonged to the estate of a lord. They had to provide labour in exchange for the use of the lord's land and his protection and justice. It was possible (but not usual) for a peasant to become a landowner, make money and even send a son to a university. But for most peasants it was hard enough just to survive.

SERFDOM

A serf, who had no rights at all, was a slave in personal bondage to a lord. Besides agricultural work, he was expected to do anything that he was ordered to do by his owner.

He was forbidden to marry outside the lord's domains so that his children would also become possessions of the noble. If he died childless, all his goods reverted to his lord.

The land-tilling peasant was at the bottom of the medieval social ladder.

HARD LIVES

Peasants and serfs spent their lives out of doors in all weathers — ploughing, planting and harvesting the fields. They milled grain, herded animals, sheared sheep and spent long hours gathering firewood in freezing weather.

Apart from paying taxes and money for the lord's ransom and his son's knighting, peasants paid for everything they used on the lord's estate — the mill for grinding corn and the ovens for baking their daily bread.

When a peasant died, the lord took his or her best possession.

The noble's fields and crops always took priority over those of the peasants; when they brought their animals back from grazing on common land, peasants had to cross the lord's fields so that they would benefit from the animals' manure.

MARKETS

Surplus crops from the manor farms were carted to the nearest towns, where they were sold at market, further enriching local nobles.

PEASANTS' REVOLTS

Some peasants saw the possibility of a better life, free from the tyranny of a greedy lord and the vagaries of the seasons. In 1358 and 1381, peasants' revolts took place in France and England when the peasantry rebelled against their hard living conditions.

To buy time the ruling kings and nobles promised to improve the peasants' living conditions, but in the end their protests were suppressed by force of arms.

WAT TYLER

A tiler by trade, Wat Tyler led a revolt against unfair working conditions and taxes in England. Together with thousands of Essex and Kentish peasants, he marched to London in 1381. The rebels were joined by more protesters and riots broke out in the streets of the city.

The 14-year-old king, Richard II, gave in to the peasants' demands and agreed to end serfdom and repressive laws in England. However, when Tyler made further demands, the Lord Mayor of London took matters into his own hands and killed the peasants' leader in front of the king. The revolt was crushed and Richard went back on his word.

End of an era

By the late 1300s, changes in society heralded the beginning of the end of the medieval era. Some of the most dramatic changes were wrought by the epidemic known as the Black Death.

> **"And nobody wept no matter what his loss because almost everyone expected death . . . and people said and believed, 'This is the end of the world'."**
>
> **A 14th-century chronicler of Siena, on the Black Death**

THE BLACK DEATH

In 1347, the Black Death, or bubonic plague, swept through Europe, killing between one-third to one-half of the total population. Vast numbers of town dwellers died in the cramped, dirty, smelly conditions in which disease-carrying fleas and rats thrived. In the countryside, whole villages were killed off and fields returned to wilderness. It was reported that the death rate in Paris was 800 people a day out of a population of only 200,000.

LABOUR SHORTAGE

Large numbers of displaced peasants gravitated towards the towns, leaving an even greater shortage of labour in the country. Almost constant warfare between England and France accelerated social changes. What the plague had failed to destroy, soldiers on both sides did their utmost to finish off. Beggars and thieves became commonplace.

IMPROVING LOT

Workers were in short supply after the plague and working wages were set at higher levels to attract them. With a smaller population, less food was needed and prices dropped accordingly.

Large landowners could no longer rely on cheap or unpaid labour on their farms because workers could find a better living elsewhere.

Laws and punishments created to deter labourers from moving proved to be unenforceable because of the numbers involved.

USING MONEY

Property and land rents were increasingly paid in money rather than in kind. Merchants and craftsmen benefited from richer workers with more disposable income.

They were able to expand their businesses, employing more workers and creating an alternative to a hard life on the land. With a smaller population, workmen were less worried about seeking better deals for themselves.

As a result of this new mobility, the rigid social boundaries and controls built into the feudal system began to blur, and the path was cleared for the changes that allowed society to evolve into the modern world.

A major theme in 14th-century art and literature was that death comes to all, from the highest to the lowest. Here, Death leads a king, bishop, nobles and peasants to their graves.

A FRAGMENTED CHURCH

The unity of the Christian Church began to crack in the 14th century, paving the way for later reforms.

In 1309, the Papacy was set up by the King of France in the town of Avignon in Provence. This caused a "Great Schism" (religious split) in the unity of Christian countries. Charges and claims of heresy were thrown back and forth between warring countries and even different regions within one state. At one point there were three rival popes.

The Church suffered a form of "privatization" originating in Avignon, which gave licences to travelling monks and friars to allow them to sell written pardons for people's sins. This became a way of raising extra funds to support the new Papacy away from its historic power base in Rome. Selling pardons was very popular, but eventually Church reformers came to see it for what it was – a corruption of everything the Church stood for and a cynical exploitation of religious power. This was the beginning of the end for a single Christian Church, which had dominated all aspects of life for the previous 700 years.

THE PLAGUE

• The Black Death, or bubonic plague, originates in China and travels west along trade routes

• There are two forms of disease: one infects the bloodstream through flea-bites; the other infects the lungs and is spread by saliva and coughing

• 1347 – the plague hits Europe. In Venice, 70% of the population die. It spreads north through France to Britain and Scandinavia

• Although doctors have no cure, some measures such as cleaning rubbish from streets and shutting infected people away help stop the plague spreading

• Victims of plague are buried in mass graves and covered in quicklime

• By 1350, about one-third of the population of Europe – about 20 million people – have died

• The word "quarantine" comes from an Italian measure to prevent a renewed outbreak of the plague in the 1370s. Suspected sailors are isolated on an island for *quaranta giorni* (40 days) to make sure they are not carrying the disease

Glossary

abbey A building or buildings occupied by monks or nuns under an abbot or abbess, or a church that was once an abbey or part of it (e.g. Westminster Abbey).

archer A bowman employed in the English armies. These men caused great slaughter on medieval battlefields and were chiefly responsible for the end of the knight as an effective fighter.

cathedral The main church in a diocese. Towns are classed as cities when they have a cathedral.

city A large town created a city by the grant of a royal charter or because it contained a cathedral within its walls.

courtier A nobleman who attended a sovereign's court on a regular basis — the forerunner of a government official.

crossbow A powerful small bow mounted across a stock, with a groove for a small arrow (bolt). The arrow was released by pulling a trigger. The weapon needed a winding mechanism in order to draw back the bow.

demesne Manor or land granted to a noble and occupied by him and his family.

Domesday Book The name given to the book that recorded the ownership of all land and property in England in 1086. This giant record was made by the order of King William I.

dowry Property or money that came with a bride upon marriage. This usually became part of the husband's estate unless legally tied up by the bride's father.

excommunicate To exclude a person from participation in the sacraments of the church. In medieval times people believed that this punishment guaranteed an eternity in hell if it was not lifted before death.

fealty Feudal tenant's faithfulness to his lord. This was usually acknowledged by a ceremony — the oath of fealty — in which the tenant swore to uphold and support his lord in all things.

feudal system Medieval system of government in Europe, based on the relative dependency of a vassal (tenant) being granted land by a lord.

freeman A peasant who was not a serf or a slave and who could sell his labour for his own benefit in town or country. He had the right to own land under a lord of his own choosing.

guild	A society founded by a group of people employed in the same trade for mutual aid and protection. There were many different guilds in medieval times, each representing different occupations. These organizations were the forerunners of trade unions.
heresy	An opinion contrary to the doctrine of the Christian Church. It was dangerous to support a heresy (or heretic) in medieval times since one of the punishments was being burnt at the stake.
mercenary	A hired soldier fighting for money or other financial reward. These soldiers were commonly employed during the Hundred Years War between England and France.
pagan	A person who was not a Christian, and believed in the old earth and sky gods. In the Middle Ages, many European people were Christians in name only; they still took care not to offend the "old gods".
papacy	The court and administration that surrounded the Pope (Latin *papa*) first situated in Rome. It relocated to Avignon in the early 14th century.
parapet	The top of a castle or city wall used to conceal and protect soldiers on a walkway.
parish	An area with its own church and clergy.
passion play	A play acted out by the ordinary people, which portrayed Christ's life and miracles.
pilgrimage	A journey undertaken by someone as an act of religious devotion.
ransom	Sum of money used to pay for the release of a prisoner.
sanctuary	A church or holy place where a fugitive from the law, or a debtor, could find refuge from arrest or violence.
serf	Person who belonged to a manor farm and fields, and whose service could be transferred from one owner to another.
sheriff	An official in charge of the law. A sheriff was responsible for administering justice under direction of the courts within a county.
squire	Member of the noble class, an attendant to a knight.
village	Group of houses, larger than a hamlet, but smaller than a town. A medieval village had a church; a hamlet did not.

PICTURE CREDITS

Bibliothèque Nationale Paris/AKG London:
24
Bibliothèque Nationale Paris/The Art
Archive: 17, 20-21, 22
British Library London/The Art Archive: 10,
18-19
Michael Dalder/Reuters/Popperfoto: 15
Dagli Orti/The Art Archive: 12-13
Whilst every attempt has been made to
clear copyright should there be any
inadvertent omission please apply in the
first instance to the publisher regarding
rectification.